# AMONG US

## Psychology Guide

COPYRIGHT

Among Us: Psychology Guide

Copyright @2021

All Rights Reserved.

The following Book is reproduced below with the goal of providing information that is as accurate and as reliable as possible. Regardless, purchasing this eBook can be seen as consent to the fact that both the publisher and the author are void of any and all liabilities.

This declaration is deemed fair and valid by both the American Bar Association and the Committee of Publishers Association and is legally binding throughout the United States.

Furthermore, the transmission, duplication, or reproduction of any of the following work, including precise information, will be considered an illegal act, irrespective of whether it is done electronically or in print. The legality extends to creating a secondary or tertiary copy of the work or a recorded copy and is only allowed with the express written consent of the Publisher. All additional rights are reserved.

The information in the following pages is broadly considered to be a truthful and accurate account of facts, and as such, any inattention, use, or misuse of the information in question by the reader will render any resulting actions solely under their purview. There are no scenarios in which the publisher or the original author of this work can be in any fashion deemed liable for any hardship or damages that may befall them after undertaking the information described herein.

Additionally, the information found on the following pages is intended for informational purposes only and should thus be considered universal. As befitting its nature, the information presented is without assurance regarding its continued validity or interim quality. Trademarks that mentioned are done without written consent and can in no way be considered an endorsement from the trademark holder.

# TABLE OF CONTENTS

INTRODUCTION: HISTORY OF AMONG US.............................................1

    AMONG US: BEGINNER'S GUIDE ON HOW TO PLAY.............................................5

HOW PSYCHOLOGICAL MANIPULATION MAKES THE GAME BETTER. .............................................9

    AMONG US' NAMES, LIES, & CHAT MAKES PLAYING FUN .............................................11

THE THEORIES OF AMONG US. .............................................13

    THE POSSIBLE ORIGINS OF IMPOSTORS .............................................14

AMONG US AND THE PSYCHOLOGY OF SOCIAL DEDUCTION. .......19

HOW PSYCHOLOGY CAN HELP YOU. .............................................23

    CHANGE THE NARRATIVE: .............................................25
    TELL THEM SWEET LITTLE LIES: .............................................28
    TAKE ADVANTAGE OF COGNITIVE MODELLING: .............................................31
    PAY IT FORWARD: .............................................34

AMONG US: BEING A SMOOTH CRIMINAL. .............................................38

    THE IMPOSTOR'S GUIDE TO SMOOTH CRIMINALITY .............................................42
    7 WAYS. .............................................46

IMPOSTORS WILL NOT SEE THIS COMING. .............................................57

    THE PSYCHOLOGICAL MIND GAMES OF AMONG US .............................................58
    HOW TO BAMBOOZLE IMPOSTORS IN AMONG US .............................................60
    WANT VOICE CHAT IN AMONG US? PLAY WITH BLUESTACKS THEN .............................................62
    AMONG US: MORE IMPORTANT TIPS AND TRICKS FOR CREWMATES AND IMPOSTERS .............................................64
    AFTER A KILL, FIND AN ALIBI .............................................68
    TRY BUDDYING UP WITH YOUR FELLOW IMPOSTER .............................................69

- Keep track of the number of survivors ............................................................. 70
- Keep sabotaging as a ghost ............................................................................. 70
- Kill in a crowd, or when crewmates are completing tasks ................... 72
- Memorize the maps' tasks................................................................................. 73
- Play with friends and use Discord.................................................................. 74
- Kick out false accusers ..................................................................................... 75
- Be ready to betray your fellow imposter....................................................... 76

# CONCLUSION: WHY AMONG US IS SO SUCCESSFUL. ...................... 77

- Mind Games ........................................................................................................ 77
- A Simple Premise ............................................................................................... 79
- Explosive Popularity........................................................................................... 80

# INTRODUCTION: HISTORY OF AMONG US.

As far as art mediums go, video games have always been unique in what they reveal about their audiences. Their interactivity provides for endless potential situations with which we can analyze the human psyche and what we know about human behavior.

If you played the popular party game Mafia, then Among Us seems familiar. InnerSloth wanted to adapt this game for mobile devices to play locally with friends. In 2018, Among Us launched with a single map and only the ability to play the game with those around you. Somewhere around 50 people would play at a time when the game first launched. Many at InnerSloth wondered if the game was a flop, but they knew they wanted to keep it going for its small but dedicated fans. This led to adding online multiplayer, new tasks, and more features to make the game more expansive.

A few months after its mobile release, the game released on Steam and featured cross-play. New maps came to the game for a low price of $4. That would later turn to free when mid-2020 saw the meteoric rise of the game's popularity and player base thanks to COVID-19 and some gaming influencers.

Soon, players can explore a fourth map that is bigger and believed to bring in unique twists to the game. The map is based on Henry Stickmin, a flash game series created by InnerSloth. If you want to see what new features and challenges the upcoming map will bring to the table, try Breaking the Bank, an HTML5 version of one of the games in the series.

The tiny indie game Among Us has risen exponentially in popularity. In this game, a group of 4 to 10 players are astronauts trapped in a broken space station. Their goal is to roam around the station and complete a multitude of simple tasks to repair the space station and win the game. The thing is, among the group lie 1 to 3 imposters, whose goal is to kill everyone else on board. They can sabotage areas of the ship to manipulate the situation and prevent players from finishing their tasks. And naturally the primary way imposters can kill others is through pressing the kill button when in their vicinity. They're also able to fast travel through vents located all over the spaceship. The innocent crewmates must win either by completing all the tasks before they're all dead, or voting out and successfully ejecting the imposters. When one comes across a dead body, they have the option to report it and everyone discusses what happened and who should be voted out, if anyone. Imposters are able to both report bodies and often may manipulate the others into voting out innocents whom they framed. There is also a button located on the map that each crewmate can press once at any time to begin the voting period.

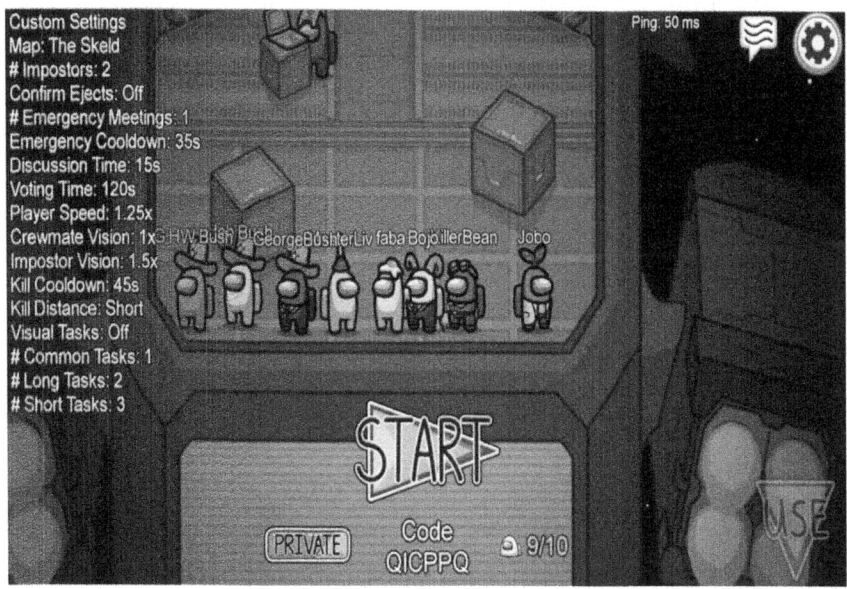

This genre of gameplay, similar to Mafia, One Night Werewolf, Town of Salem, Push the Button, and more, is unique in that players must embody the strategic mindset of detectives and imposters, with a heavy emphasis on discussion, manipulation, and strategic skills. Players of course are aware that it's just a game, they aren't actually killing anyone, and are free to mess around, which many do, but truly most of the gameplay causes them to build many of the same skills and strategies that real life detectives, investigators, and criminals utilize. Players practice memorizing alibis, paying attention to details in reference to time frame, and avoiding blaming others too strongly for suspicious actions yet still knowing to keep an extra eye on them. They practice making proper use of bluffing, tone of voice, when to talk and when not to talk, when and when not to trust witness testimony, and how to cover up common mistakes. They learn both how to gain others trust, and how to convince others to lose all trust in someone. They practice how to manipulate the crowd, confuse the situation, stall for time, track personal player habits, and catch each other's uses of all of these strategies.

This free mobile cartoon game made by a team of three people in a couple months is a prime example of how games give people of all ages the opportunity to practice specific strategies that they would normally almost never need and/or should practice elsewhere. And as an aspiring game designer myself, I find this incredibly inspiring. It serves as a prime example of the unique potential that games have to teach and educate, while also being genuinely entertaining. Both for players and for those interested in human psychology, video games are becoming more of a tool to understanding how we respond to specific situations and why.

# Among Us: Beginner's Guide On How To Play.

Even though Among Us has been out for quite a while, it seemingly exploded with popularity overnight. Most recently, the player count in Among Us even peaked higher than PUBG momentarily. With all these new players coming into the game, it might help to have a basic guide for how to play, and the answers to some of the questions many new players ask.

The basic overview of Among Us is simple. A crew of 4-10 (usually 10) players are at a location doing tasks while 1-3 impostors (usually 2) are doing everything they can to sabotage their efforts and kill them all. The game ends in one of four ways.

1. All impostors are dead. (Crew Win)

2. All tasks are completed. (Crew Win)

3. There are an equal number of crew and impostors. (Impostor Win)

4. The crew fail to stop a catastrophic sabotage (Impostor Win)

Games can be longer or shorter based on the number of players, their skills, and the options selected by the play group. When a game starts, you will be assigned a role, either as crew or impostors, and your goals and how you achieve them will change based on that.

For that purpose, the crew and impostor sections will be separated.

When you are a member of Among Us that means you're out there to help repair this ship/station/colony. For every game as Crew, you'll be assigned tasks listed in your task list. You can locate where to do these tasks on the map. Simply walk over to each location and complete the job. Some jobs are going to be harder than others, but you'll eventually figure them out. Don't be afraid to ask your fellow crewmates how to do some of your tasks if you have to, it's all part of learning on the job.

Of course, there may be some impostors Among Us, so keep an eye out for suspicious activity. Impostors don't do tasks, but they might fake it. You can keep an eye on the task list to keep track of every task that is completed, and if you think you see something suspicious, you can always call a meeting using the button on the table.

But most of the time, you might not see anything suspicious at all. If you end up alone with an impostor, you might find yourself becoming a ghost. Just because you're dead doesn't mean your job is finished though, so make sure to do your tasks and count on your crewmates to solve your death.

When you get assigned Impostor, you get to sabotage the Among Us Crew. That means you'll be in charge of throwing a wrench into their operations, and making sure this job is anything but "business as usual."

On your screen, you'll see a list of tasks and their locations on the map, but these are just suggestions for things to fake and not your actual goal. Instead, you'll want to try to find a way to isolate members of the Crew and kill them whenever you can. Of course, this won't be easy, and you'll have to be sneaky.

Fortunately there are a few crawlspaces for you to use, usually covered up by vent coverings. You'll want to use your mobility to your advantage as you pick off the crew one by one.

But there are other things you can do as well. If you open your sabotage map you'll see there are quite a few things you can do. You can lock doors to keep the crew stuck, or break the lights and limit their vision.

You can also sabotage their communications, preventing them from seeing their tasks. Additionally, you can sabotage the reactors, oxygen, or other vital pieces of equipment that will spell doom for everyone unless they're fixed.

What to do when a meeting is called? Meetings are the only times players have to talk with each other, making them an important part of Among Us. Meetings get called when a body is reported, or when someone presses the emergency meeting button.

If you're the crew, use this opportunity to share information and interrogate suspects. If you're an impostor, use this time to throw off suspicion and sow chaos.

At each meeting, players can vote to execute one person, and if anyone has the most votes then they will be thrown out of an airlock/into a volcano.

If you don't want to vote someone off, however, you can also vote to skip at the bottom. Use the meeting time wisely, as communication will be vital to helping the crew coordinate, and equally as important for impostors to disrupt.

# HOW PSYCHOLOGICAL MANIPULATION MAKES THE GAME BETTER.

Among Us is an online multiplayer game that requires players to use their skills at deduction, or deceit, in order to achieve victory. This game features lobbies of up to 10 people, most of which will become Crewmates who have a series of tasks they must complete. The few left over are given the role of Imposter, and they must eliminate the Crewmates in order to win. The main defense against the Imposters is the vote screen, which can be initiated upon finding the body of a Crewmate, or by hitting the emergency button located somewhere on the map. This is where Among Us becomes a psychological game, as Imposters have votes too, and a good enough Imposter might even be able to convince Crewmates to vote out their own comrades.

Anyone who has played Town of Salem, Deceit, Garry's Mod, and a host of other games knows that sometimes innocents are their own worst enemy. The same is true for Among Us, especially in public games, as sometimes something as simple as having a funny name can get someone off scot-free. The in-game Among Us text chat is a big contributor to this, as it allows players and Imposters to communicate in the same space. Imposters can use this text chat feature, or even voice chat if people are using alternate apps for communication, to manipulate Crewmates into trusting them, doubting their friends, or sometimes even liking them too much to vote them out. After all, who could vote out someone named Trusty Bob? Trusty is literally in their name!

The psychological manipulation in Among Us is actually part of what makes the game so great. In the best cases it can even begin to feel like John Carpenter's The Thing, where nobody is free of suspicion and even the person taking charge could be lying about their identity. In games like these, especially in bigger lobbies with the confirm ejects option off, Imposters can do their best work at spinning up lies and nailing the blame onto other players. Funnily enough, this actually doesn't make playing a Crewmate less fun. In fact, seeing through the Imposter's lies and becoming a kind of Sherlock Holmes is one of the best parts of the game. Even getting eliminated as a Crewmate isn't too bad, as one can still help out by completing tasks in ghost form.

# AMONG US' NAMES, LIES, & CHAT MAKES PLAYING FUN

Among Us has become an extremely popular title as of late, and for good reason. After all, it isn't every game that lets players pop out of a vent, immediately murder their best friend, report the body, and then blame it all on someone innocent who was actually about to report that they saw the player do the deed. It's interactions like these that prove how psychological manipulation in Among Us isn't only a core game mechanic, but that it's also a main factor in the game's fun.

It's unavoidable that good Imposters in Among Us need to play mind games with Crewmates somehow. After all, a game where the Imposter simply admits to their in-game crimes would be boring, especially for the Crewmates, who wouldn't have gotten the satisfaction of solving the mystery on their own. It's for this reason that the game actually seems to benefit from psychological manipulation. It might sound bad, and in almost any case outside of being part of a game it is a bad thing to do, but the mental gymnastics that go on in Among Us are one of the things that make it such an enjoyable game to play with both friends and strangers.

# THE THEORIES OF AMONG US.

Among Us' dastardly Impostors terrorize crewmates with various forms of killing and sabotage, and fans have theories about their origins and motives.

The Impostors that give Among Us its name and central gameplay hook are, by design, a mysterious bunch. On the surface, they're nearly identical to Among Us' colorful crewmates, but Impostors exhibit certain strange and terrifying properties. Due to the game's lack of overt story, it's unclear what exactly Among Us' Impostors are, but fans have a few compelling theories.

Unlike normal crewmates, Impostors have the ability to slink through vents, which - unless crewmates are small enough to do this, too, but simply have no need to - suggests they have some kind of shapeshifting ability. This would also explain Impostors' ability to open up a large mouth at the waist of their spacesuits and stab victims with sharp tongues. It's possible Among Us' crewmates also have mouths hidden there, and the Impostor only uses this horrifying ability because of some malicious motive. Since no other crewmates are seen doing this, though, it seems unlikely.

Knowing Impostors possess these unique properties, Among Us fans have naturally tried to figure out exactly what Impostors are and where they came from. Although the exact nature of their biology is hard to determine without clearer statements from developer InnerSloth, there's still much fans can glean about Impostors' intelligence and origins.

## The Possible Origins Of Impostors

As explained in a theory by Apex Legends YouTuber KEVTHEKING99-YT, the Impostors, whatever they are, appear to have come from Polus, a planet that hosts the Among Us map of the same name. The crewmates' research there seems to have gone wrong, resulting in either the escape of a shapeshifting specimen that mimics crewmates or an infection that turns them into Impostors. Since Impostors leave behind half-devoured crewmate corpses, KEVTHEKING99-YT theorizes they are essentially just animals, attempting to feed and survive through camouflage, as some Earth predators do.

One potential problem with this theory is Among Us' Impostors exhibit more intelligence than traditionally associated with animals. They are able to deliberately sabotage crewmates' tasks and perform their own fake tasks, so they seem to have at least some awareness of the crewmates' goals. Perhaps, then, the parasites or shape-shifters are intelligent creatures. The lengths they goes in order to eliminate entire crews might give more insight into this intelligence, too: Rather than opportunistic hunters looking for a quick meal, Impostors could have a purposeful vendetta against crewmates, attacking them in retaliation for invading their home planet.

One darker theory, from Reddit user I_exist_YaYY, suggests there might not even be a real Impostor. According to the theory, a paranoid crewmate, spurred on by horror stories of a shapeshifting enemy, begins to suspect others are Impostors and secretly kills them in an attempt to protect the crew, thus unwittingly becoming the Impostor themselves. This, of course, wouldn't explain the big mouth, sharp tongue, or half-eaten bodies, but maybe the would-be savior's deteriorating mental state leads them to hallucinate such horrific killings. Still, this theory seems less likely than the others, so it's safer to assume Among Us' Impostors really are some kind of vengeful, alien body-snatchers from Polus.

According to an established consensus, the following set of theories are widely believed to be common knowledge.

I.   All of the crewmates are Imposters.

According to a theory by Screenrant, all of the players in the game are shape-shifting aliens: "Perhaps the violent Impostors in 'Among Us' are a result of a genetic mutation, and once confined with other Crewmates, they turn into killers. The possibilities are really endless..." It seems that if they are confined to a tight space, or reach a certain age, certain aliens just can't handle the pressure and start killing their crewmates.

II.    The Player will always lose.

It is impossible to win "Among Us." "Game Theory" states, "This is a game where canonically, you lose. Your best interrogation skills, your mastery of 900 IQ stats, your sussing out of the most sus suspects: all for nothing. You will die. Your friends will die. Your loved ones will all die. There is no winning in "Among Us."

He goes on to explain that the game may seem fair but discovers that no matter where you play the game—The Skeld, MIRA HQ and Polus—the imposters come back. Meaning, that you never got rid of them in the first place. You will fail to get rid of them, and they will come back to your home planet and kill the population. "You may have thought that you won, but as the game title says: the alien imposters are still among us." No matter what you do, the imposters will follow you to previously safe locations.

# AMONG US AND THE PSYCHOLOGY OF SOCIAL DEDUCTION.

Social deduction games are highly immersive and intellectually stimulating experiences where players attempt to resolve and uncover the hidden roles, motives, and allegiances of the other members.

Usually, such games are played within teams, where the main members are primarily the "good" ones and the impostors are the "bad" ones.

During such games, players may have to use their superb skills of deduction and logic to make sense of the roles of others, even when those other players are unreliable. The impostors may utilize elaborate and well-padded bluffs to keep the suspicion away from themselves.

The impostors may even go as far as gaslighting others to absolve themselves of their so-called misdeeds. Others may capitalize on the drama between two innocents to detract away from their own conniving schemes.

When you're the impostor, there are many strategies to keep yourself from getting caught. These may include:

1. Sticking to a specific story consistently with conviction

2. Producing a fake alibi with actual innocents or a fellow impostor

3. Pretending to be too new to understand the complexities of the game

4. Obtaining critical information at the right time and the right place

5. Running away from the scene of the crime

6. Additional research on the various strategies of the game.

All social deduction games generally follow a similar pattern: players are secretly separated into teams and one team has to identify the other. The exact theme or flavor of those teams varies from game to game, and the limitations on what is possible depends heavily on whether it's played online or in person.

For example, Town of Salem and Among Us have certain freedoms not available to games like Secret Hitler, and as a result the games focus on different aspects of social deduction.

Additionally, while the tools used by both teams can vary game to game, they all have communication as a central part of gameplay.

In Among Us, the tools for imposters include sabotages and kills, while crewmates have tasks as a source of inevitability. Secret Hitler gives fascists the ability to coordinate powers, while liberals outnumber them, and they must compete for special one-time-use presidential powers.

The biggest separation in social deduction games is between those that are more action oriented and those that are more meeting oriented. Among Us falls clearly within the action oriented games, or those in which the players are expected to perform actions throughout the game, with limited meeting or coordination time available.

This can be seen in the way that Among Us players have to fulfil tasks, and physically move around a 2D space in order to gather evidence about their location.

Town of Salem and Secret Hitler exist at the opposite end of that spectrum, with all or a majority of the game time used for meetings where players can communicate their information and attempt to coordinate. In this case, the goal is for the innocent team (town, liberals) to stop the other team before they can achieve their goals.

Of course, Among Us doesn't just get played one way. Players also have the option of using the highly customizable options to gear the game towards how they want to play it. If you want to deemphasize the actionable parts of the game you can increase view distance, add on a ton of tasks, and increase the kill cool downs.

If you'd rather play a game that is more about using the actionable parts of Among Us, such as sabotages and moving through the map, then you can reduce kill cooldowns and view distances to allow for more action to take place.

But regardless of how you want to play, Among Us is a great entry into the social deduction genre of games.

# HOW PSYCHOLOGY CAN HELP YOU.

Although it's been around for more than two years now, it's only been in the past couple of months that InnerSloth's space-themed social deduction game, Among Us, has exploded into popularity, topping Twitch charts on an almost-daily basis and getting a lot more attention over on YouTube. Based on the real-life party game Mafia and the product of a three-person team, the game released to very little fanfare (or even attention, really), but its recent surge in popularity – it's gone from having "fewer than 30-50 players per hour" at release to "70,000-110,000 per hour" toward the end of August – has seen InnerSloth cancel the sequel it was planning to release so that it could focus on improving its newfound cultural phenomenon.

Among Us sees a group of up to ten crew members working together to complete a series of tasks to prepare a space station for launch, all the while trying to uncover the identity of an impostor (or impostors), who goes around the station attempting to kill the crewmates. Whenever a member of the crew finds and reports a dead body, the players can use the in-game messaging function – or better yet, a Discord call – to try and figure out who the killer amongst them (haha, get it?) might be. The crew then votes on who they believe is the impostor, and the person with the most votes gets removed from the game whether they were the killer or not. The crew members win the game if they correctly expose the impostors or complete the tasks set out to them; the impostor or impostors win if they manage to kill everyone. Given that it'll only run you AU$7.50 on Steam and it's free on mobile, it's easy to access and easy to learn... but very difficult to master.

The state of Victoria is in its second lengthy lockdown period, so Among Us has become the arena in which my friends and I have our weekly game nights. Instead of doing anything that vaguely resembles actual productivity outside of those game nights, though, I've focused my attention on ensuring that I win every single game for the foreseeable future (if you're reading this, Luke, go to hell). The internal is full of guides on how to best approach being a crewmate or the impostor, but I've got something even better than that: I've got psychology, and even though I know my own friends will see this, I'm going to share the techniques I've been using because they're sure to increase your win percentage — when they do, remember you found them on Doublejump.

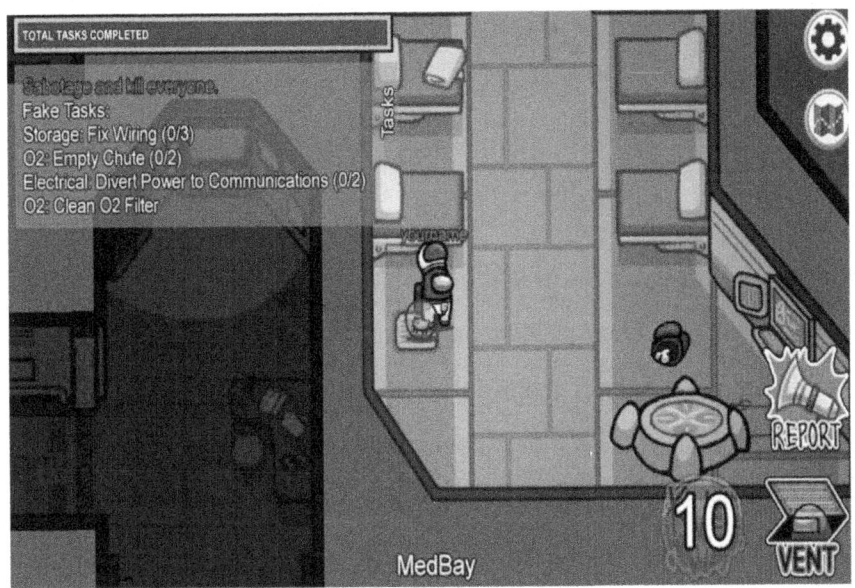

# CHANGE THE NARRATIVE:

At its core, Among Us is about witness testimony and memory. Fortunately or unfortunately, human memory is incredibly easy to manipulate; thousands of studies have consistently shown that it's possible to implant ideas in participants' memories simply by altering the questions and statements you use when exploring them. One of the most famous examples of this is that of Loftus and Palmer (1974), who showed their participants a video of a car accident and then gave them a questionnaire, with one of the questions asking how fast the cars were going when they "hit" each other. Subsequent groups received the same questionnaire, but with the verb "hit" switched out for words like "bumped", "collided", "contacted" and "smashed". Loftus and Palmer found that the choice of verb in the questionnaire appeared to influence the participants' perception of how quickly the car was moving: those who saw the verb "contacted", for instance, estimated that the cars were moving at 51.2km/h, while those who saw the word "smashed" estimated that they were doing 65.7km/h — a considerable difference.

That in itself may not seem useful in this context, but the experiment had a second phase to it. A week later, Loftus and Palmer followed up with the participants, asking them a single question: "did you see any broken glass?" The video itself did not show any broken glass (as surprising as that may be in itself), but the participants who had the verb "smashed" in their questionnaire a week earlier — as opposed to something like "hit" or "collided with" — reported that they had seen broken glass. This suggests that the verbs themselves had at least some impact in modifying and distorting the participants' memories; of course, the one-week delay may have played a part as well, but in a high-stress situation like a game of Among Us, memories are more prone to lapses and therefore, more prone to manipulation. That brings us to how we can apply this theory in Among Us.

In this hypothetical, we're in a game where Blue has called a meeting in which they're casting suspicion on their crewmate, Orange, but Red is the actual impostor. Some guides would recommend that Red just stay quiet and let Blue and Orange argue with one another, eating up the discussion time, not arousing any suspicion and potentially letting either Blue or Orange say something that gets them suspected. That's a perfectly valid strategy, for sure, but there's a more "aggressive" option: Red could align themselves with a crewmate, let's say Green, while completing the tasks, at the same time keeping an eye on other players.

In the meeting, Red could then ask Green a leading question like "how fast do you think Orange/Blue was going when they darted past us?" or "how long do you think Orange/Blue was waiting when they snuck in behind us?" These types of questions imply that Orange or Blue has done a certain thing, but because that intention isn't overtly obvious, they will often plant the idea in Green's mind — and Green's corroboration of that question will plant the thought in the other crewmates' minds. Red can even repeat the strategy later on in the game because a crewmate won't typically notice a well-presented leading question unless they're looking for it; as a crewmate, the best way to pick this strategy out is simply to be looking out for it. Additionally, keep your own questions more general, asking things like "what can you tell us?" rather than "did you see when X did Y?", as this reduces the sway that leading questions can have.

## Tell Them Sweet Little Lies:

Leading questions are hard to pull off without getting caught out, both in Among Us and in real-world applications. What isn't so difficult to pull off, though, is simple misinformation, and it just so happens that Johnson and Seifert (1994), among many others, have shown that humans have a very difficult time negating the influence of misinformation, even if it's retracted immediately afterward. Johnson and Seifert split their participants into three groups and told each group a story about a warehouse fire caused by short-circuiting in a storage closet, which differed ever-so-slightly between the three groups: they told the first group (the control group) that the closet where the fire started was empty; they told the second group that there were flammable items in the closet, and then retracted that information immediately; and they told the third group that there were flammable items in the closet but waiting until much later on to retract that information. After telling the story to each group, Johnson and Seifert then had them complete a questionnaire about the fire, testing what they thought caused it. The control group attributed the fire to the faulty wiring, while the other two groups both attributed it to the flammable items – despite the fact that that information had been retracted.

Applying this principle to Among Us is quite simple. In this hypothetical game, Blue has reported finding a body and everyone is asking the customary who and where questions, except Cyan isn't talking. The impostor, good old Red, can call attention to Cyan's silence, casting an inkling of suspicion on them (but not enough to make it obvious) and immediately follow up with a "just kidding". Alternatively, Red can use the same logic to suggest that Blue self-reported finding the body, watch Blue get flustered, act out and create a self-fulfilling prophecy that leads everyone to suspect them... and then take it back. If Blue still hasn't been thrown out later in the game, Red can repeat the tactic and/or call attention back to Blue's actions throughout the game. Here's an example of how this strategy played out in one of my own games; in this context, Cyan is adamant that they saw Red kill Purple, but the other impostor and myself were able to cast doubt on both players. In the following rounds, Red and then Cyan got voted off, which allowed Orange and I to win the game.

There's an important caveat with this strategy, though: it'll only work if you've already earned a couple of other players' trust — Among Us motivates players to question everything, which is one of the key ways to negate the effects of misinformation, so you're going to be better off if fewer people have a reason to question your lies. Orange and I got lucky in the example above, because Cyan and Red were motivated to ignore facts and accuse each other, which allowed us to manipulate poor Brown. Additionally, it's important to note that if you're on the receiving end of this strategy, just saying that you're not guilty and putting your word against someone who's gotten a few crewmates to trust them is not going to cut it; people want an explanation, so the best defence against misinformation is to stick with another crewmate at all times so that they can corroborate your side. Alternatively, just keep your cool if someone accuses you, because you know the truth and they'll slip up first. Whatever you do, just don't pull a Red. That'll just make you look more suspicious.

# TAKE ADVANTAGE OF COGNITIVE MODELLING:

Of course, impostors can also win by simply convincing everyone else that their arguments are true, and there are two effective, somewhat foolproof methods through which to achieve that — and I believe I know when it's best to use each one. Social psychology suggests that the way an individual presents an argument has an influence on attitude and behavioural change. The Elaboration Likelihood Model proposes that there are two major ways in which individuals consider the content of a message: the central route, which considers a lot more cognitive information like the quality of the argument, individual motivation and how important the decision is; and the peripheral route, which comes into play when the individual isn't motivated or doesn't have enough time to engage with the message. That peripheral route is also subject to mental heuristics, such as the quantity of arguments.

## Elaboration Likelihood Model

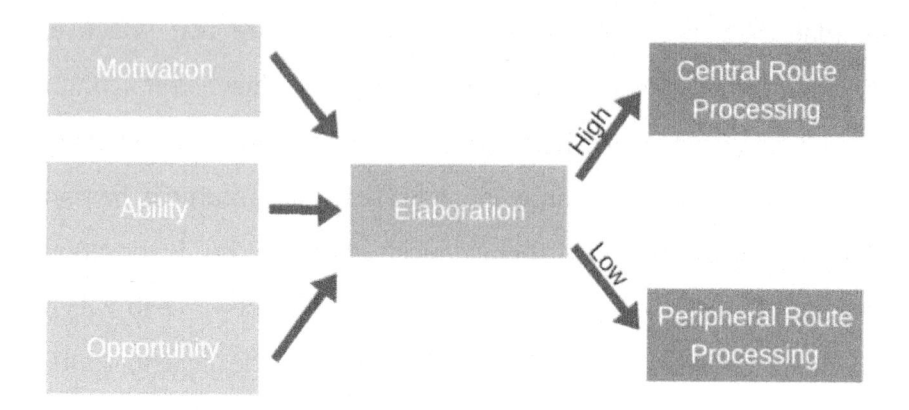

A schematic diagram of the Elaboration Likelihood Model.

Throughout my time with Among Us, I've noticed that the later it gets in the game, the less likely the crew is to throw someone out. This makes sense when you consider the game's mechanics. Early on in the game, the crew outnumbers the impostor(s) by quite a bit, and its chances of winning increase dramatically if they manage to eject an impostor early. On the other hand, as the game wears on and there are fewer people left, people are less confident in their ideas because the wrong decision could mean an instant game over. When considering this, the impostor's optimal play becomes obvious — cast as much doubt as possible into other players' minds and encourage early ejections whenever they can. Early in the game, people don't have a lot of motivation to critically engage with any evidence presented for a number of reasons: it's easy enough to just pop into another game if they make a mistake early on and get ejected; there are too many crewmates talking over one another so it's difficult to make a coherent point; and, of course, the time limit forces everyone into quick decisions. The impostor(s) can therefore take advantage of the early game, overwhelm the other crewmates with argument quantity rather than quality, and get a few players out the airlock.

Of course, the simplest strategy is also the one that fails the easiest. As you get further into the game, crewmates have more of an opportunity to contribute to the discussion because there are fewer people involved in it, and they're more motivated to engage with arguments critically because they can see their win in sight. If you're the impostor and you get to this point, the crew will likely be more motivated to create a strategy – like a buddy system – to limit the impostor's killing opportunities,

you should focus on giving yourself an alibi and relying on sabotage to separate members of the crew. If that doesn't help and you can feel an ejection coming on, you shouldn't try to argue your way out of it: the crew is smarter towards the endgame, so a more optimal play would be to suggest that you aim for a "task win" instead, citing what happens if the crew makes the wrong call.

This strategy is based on cognitive modelling, so the best way to combat the strategy would be to have read this article and know about these processing models – that way, you can call them out and cast suspicion where it belongs. Failing that, just don't entertain baseless accusations like "Red seems sus" without asking why Red seems sus. It might seem like common sense, but one only needs to spend an hour playing Among Us to know just how successful this strategy can be for an impostor.

# Pay it forward:

If you're planning to employ these strategies the next time you're cast as the impostor, bear in mind that they all rely on the crew actually trusting you. You're going to do a whole lot of talking during each discussion, but it's going to mean nothing if the crew can't account for your whereabouts in the round; since you're going to be killing some people, you're going to be unaccounted for at times, so you need the crew to trust you to be alone. For that, the crew needs to like you. My favourite way to earn the crew's trust is by helping them — not in an overt sense, of course, because that would be counterintuitive, but in a more subtle way.

Recently, I played a game where myself and Black were the impostors. I didn't kill anyone when the game started, instead opting to walk with Brown and fake doing some of my tasks. When the crew found the first body, I vouched for Brown, who immediately vouched for me as well. Perfect. Pink was arguing that Black was the killer, but a little bit of misinformation caused Brown to doubt Pink's testimony, leading to a skipped vote. Immediately after the skipped vote, Black goes ahead and kills Pink, and Brown says we should vote Black out the airlock. impostors typically don't want to vote their fellow impostors out unless it would be suspicious if they didn't — it wouldn't have been suspicious in this situation, but I'd gained Brown's trust and I wanted to keep it, so I backed them up. Black then disconnected from the game, leaving four players: myself, Blue, Lime and my good mate Brown. Lime picked up on the fact that Blue wasn't active in the chat, so I used that to cast doubt away from myself and onto Blue. In hindsight, Blue was just away from the keyboard, but by this point all I needed to do was slip away, kill Lime and blame it on Blue.

The trust that I earned from Brown in that game is an example of the reciprocal norm; people feel obligated to return a favour to someone who does them a favour. In this example, Brown felt obligated to vouch for me solely because I vouched for them. Then, when I agreed with Brown about voting Black out, they viewed me as less of a suspect because, in their mind, it would be silly for me to halve my chance of winning in that way. The more players the impostor can successfully get to trust them, the less of a suspect they'll appear to be as the round progresses. Don't overdo it, though — remember, you still need to kill to win.

As a crew member in this situation, all you really need to do to beat this technique is avoid reciprocity: old Brown was blinded by their obligation to return my favour, but if they'd paid closer attention to what I was doing rather than just where I was, they would have known that I wasn't actually doing very much, but they were blinded by their obligation to reciprocate. Marry yourself to the facts — only vouch for a player when you know for a fact that they're not the killer — and you'll be able to avoid getting played for a fool like poor Brown (Brown, if you're reading this... sorry mate).

Ultimately, it would be impossible to break down all of the optimal decisions to make in Among Us, but reading this Herculean breakdown of social and cognitive psychology should give you a pretty significant edge when it comes time for a meeting. Sure, you may start to feel a little bad for messing with people's minds like that, but just remember, if you're the impostor... that's the name of the game.

Good luck in your future game nights, dear reader — may nobody suspect a thing.

# AMONG US: BEING A SMOOTH CRIMINAL.

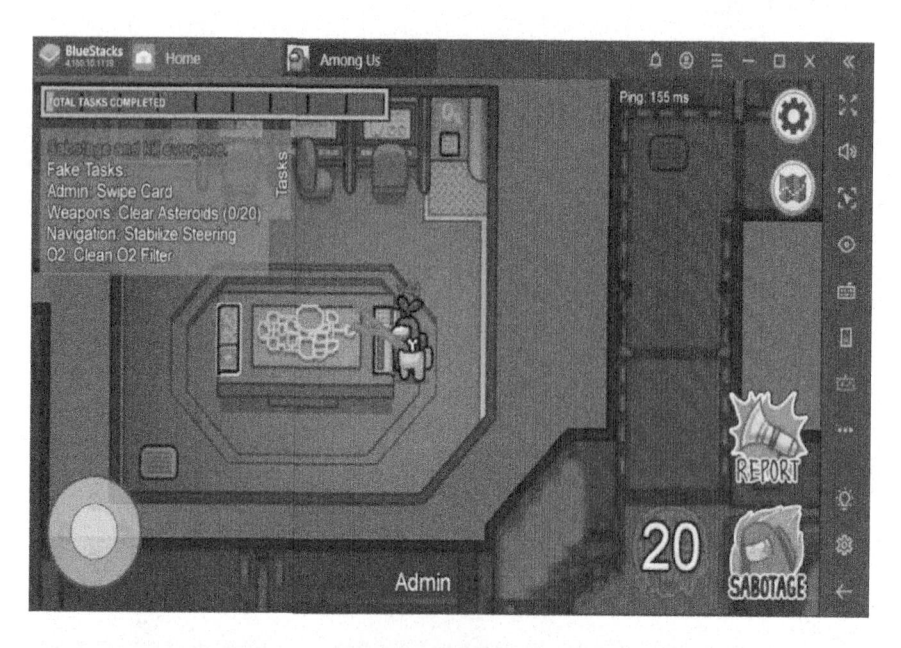

Although being a Crewmate is certainly awesome, especially when you can find a group of people who are willing to cooperate, the Impostor role is, by far, the most exhilarating one. Think of it as the game's version of a Joker character – a wildcard or loose cannon whom nobody can control and everyone has to stay away from. Unfortunately, your odds of landing in this position are quite small (25% in a match of 4 players or, more likely, 10% in a lobby of 10). In case you don't get to be an Impostor, though, don't be a downer by leaving the lobby.

Your odds might be improved depending on the host's settings, since you can have up to 3 Impostors in one game. Now that's chaos. To get the most fun out of Impostoring, you should take care to play it very carefully. Your overarching goal is to kill all Crew members before they get to complete the list of available tasks without getting voted out. You won't be able to complete any tasks yourself, but you will be given a general list of assignments you might want to fake so as to earn everybody else's trust.

Be wary, though, because not all tasks will be available for the Crew, so you might actually want to lay back and be observant for a little while. Many inexperienced Impostors try to scan their cards into the Admin station without first making sure that the task is actually available. If you play with attentive players, they'll call an emergency meeting and oust you faster than you can blink.

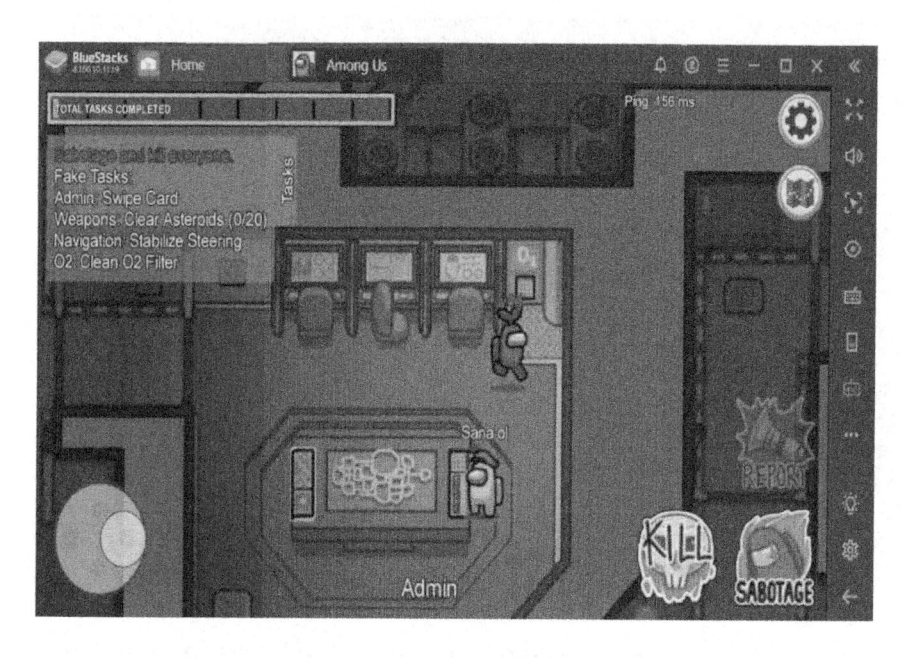

You have two abilities as an Impostor, Sabotage and Kill, and we can't seem to decide which is more fun. We'll stick with the Kill, for now. No, Sabotage. No, no. Kill. The latter gives you the possibility to slay a Crewmate when you're within range (distance can be short, medium, or long, depending on the host's settings). Usually, there's a

10 second cooldown. This can, however, be increased by the host to a full minute, should they desire a more slow-paced game.

Sabotage, on the other hand, creates a temporary problem somewhere on the ship. Depending on what it is, Crewmates might have to just wait it out, go there fix it, or ignore what's going on. You can also lock them up in various rooms for a limited amount of time by closing the doors. Lastly, Impostors can crawl through vents which are inaccessible to Crew. You can use these to either hide after a kill or move around the map with great ease. The time you spend here doesn't count towards the CD of your Sabotage or Kill, though.

# The Impostor's Guide to Smooth Criminality

1. Calm and Confidence.

You can come up with a series of excuses when someone tries to point the finger at you for trying to fake complete a task. So long as it's game related, you have a good chance of convincing the group. For example, when someone accuses you of fake asteroid killing, you can say that the system was sabotaged and the guns must have been jammed.

If you're caught next to a vent, you can claim that you noticed some fishy movements around there and were trying to check it for Impostors. Similarly, if somebody suspects you for closing doors, you can say that you were trying to prevent them for closing and that "Crewmember X" actually closed them.

## 2. Don't Jump the Gun

Believe it or not, you can get people in trouble for saying the truth if they're not careful enough to augment their statements with sound proof. For instance, if someone says they saw you going into a vent, you can easily turn it around and claim they're trying to divert attention from themselves.

As a general rule, players tend to see those who jump the gun with increased skepticism. When debating for yourself during a discussion, try to seem laid-back. You also get bonus points if you can convince the group that an emergency meeting was called for nothing – nobody hates fake emergencies more than Crewmates.

3. Don't Give Yourself Away

Certain tasks have an animation when they are being completed by a Crew member. When someone is blasting meteors, you can actually see the guns firing. Similarly, the medical bay's scan will have a green animation. Shield, as well as trash disposal assignments also have visual cues. If a group of people is formed, you want to go ahead and stick with them as much as possible, to avoid suspicion.

4. Take the Initiative

The best way to ensure victory as an Impostor in Among Us is to take the initiative. Don't let Crewmates control the game by going around in big groups. Keep sabotaging different rooms on opposite sides of the ship and divide them as much as possible. When this is feasible, go with whoever is alone. When they reach a room that also has a vent, make sure that nobody is nearby and make your move. Then, scurry off to the vent and go into a different room.

We haven't had this much fun with a mobile game in a long time, which is also part of the reason why we've spent way more evenings on it than we probably should have. Or not. Who's to say that we won't someday benefit from these social skills in real life? What if our application to Survivor is finally picked up and Jeff Probst calls us on a million-dollar adventure? We have to be prepared. Always.

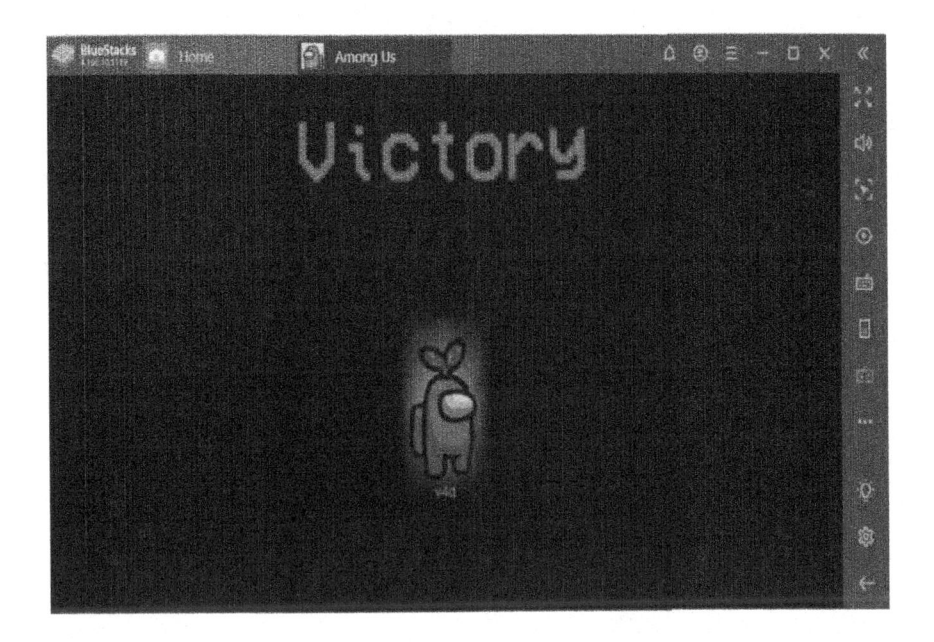

# 7 WAYS.

The game takes place in space, where players are divided into either crewmate (the good guy) or impostor (the bad guy). The crewmates must finish all their tasks or identify all the impostors in order to win while the impostors must kill all the crewmates before the taskbar finishes. Players can vote to eject suspected impostors by calling an emergency meeting.

To win the game as an impostor, you'll need to know how to manipulate people. To do so, you need to know how people work. So, here are 7 ways you can use psychology to manipulate your friends and win as the impostor in Among Us.

1. Priming: Establish your innocence early in the game

Priming theory posits that people's future thoughts and actions can be manipulated using a set of stimuli. While you obviously can't manipulate someone to do anything drastic, you can nudge them to veer towards a certain direction. By priming them early in the game, you're giving the players a foundation to base their thoughts on.

For example, let's say you're Brown. To throw suspicion off yourself, you say, "I think I saw some light colours near the body." By doing so, you're subtly taking the suspicion of yourself and associating the characters with light colours like white, yellow and light green to the murder. Regardless of whether the other players actually take the bait, you have at least planted the seed.

You can also prime someone using your action. How do you do that? Well, you start marinating. Choose an unsuspecting crewmate. Group up and stick together. If a dead body is found, claim that it could not have been you since you were with another crewmate the whole time.

To pull this tactic off, you need to act like one of the crewmates and fake your tasks. Since you'll need to stay near your marinated crewmate to gain their trust and have them vouch for you, you also need to be smarter in how you kill. Either kill only during lights out or only employ this tactic when there's a second impostor.

2. Scapegoat theory: Blame someone who doesn't easily fight back

The thing about the game is, everyone knows that there's at least one impostor. So it makes sense for everyone to be wary of one another, which makes your job as an impostor a lot harder. In order for you to win, you need to find someone you can easily shift the blame to.

How do you find the perfect scapegoat? Well, according to social psychology, humans have a tendency to shift blame to others and the scapegoats are often outliers. Find someone who's not really part of the group to become your scapegoat.

Identifying this outlier can be hard especially if you're playing with your friends. One way to do this is by pointing out players who don't move in groups throughout the game. Because players in the group cannot vouch for the scapegoat's location, it's easier to pin the murders on them.

You have to do this with tact though. Make sure to target people who don't easily fight back. A vocal scapegoat might be able to pick on what you're trying to do, automatically turning you into a suspect. When done right, scapegoats can be useful as they can really affect your likelihood of winning the game.

3. Reciprocity: Be nice and vouch for others

The norm of reciprocity in social psychology suggests that people feel obligated to reciprocate the kindness that they receive. For instance, if a friend does you a favour by printing your course notes, you're more likely to help them out if they need to borrow your laptop.

As an impostor, you can use the reciprocity principle to your advantage.

Whenever you have the chance, be nice. Vouch for someone and validate their claims. If the team suspects them, serve as their alibi. If they claim to have seen something of significance during the meeting, support their claim.

Be careful not to be too obvious. Make sure you can provide your own reasonings as to why you're vouching for the player and supporting their claims. You can say you saw the same thing they did and that you were with the player throughout the whole round so there's no way they could be the impostor.

If you do this correctly, the player may feel that you're a reliable crewmate. Once that happens, take advantage of it. Kill off the others while maintaining trust between you and the other player. If you ever get to the final standoff, the player might even believe you over their own crewmates, leading them to voting the wrong person and giving you the victory.

4. Consistency: Highlight when people are acting inconsistently

> WAIT, YOU SAID I WAS INNOCENT BEFORE? WHICH ONE IS IT?

One of the key principles of persuasion is consistency — that is, people like to be consistent with the things they have previously said and done.

How can you take advantage of this? Well, you'll want to highlight when people are being inconsistent with their stories. This is particularly useful when you've become a suspect and have been deemed innocent in the earlier rounds. Remind allies how they defended you previously and the reasons for it. Reinforce that your innocence is consistent with their inner beliefs and that if they are turning against you, perhaps they are the ones who are the impostors.

It also helps if you are also consistent with your story as people can easily detect when you are contradicting yourself. Stick to a coherent narrative so that others are more likely to believe you.

5. Projective identification: Bring attention to crewmates who have managed to win as impostors

As humans, we have a tendency to bring our feelings and assumptions from a previous relationship into a new one. We call this projective identification. You can take advantage of this principle to turn the players against each other.

Cast suspicion on crewmates who have managed to win as an impostor before. Point out how they've successfully won previously and how the team should not trust them easily. Chances are, people might agree with you. If they bite, continue to build that story. Make kills that will implicate these crewmates.

If the crewmates don't fall for it, you can still find a scapegoat by looking at the team's pool of suspects. Then, build a case against them. Your case doesn't have to be solid. It just needs to be strong enough to push for a confirmation bias. Once most of the information is there, you can easily push the team to favour the information that confirms their suspicion of the scapegoats.

6. False recognition: Ask specific questions to manipulate memory

Memories are actually not that hard to manipulate. According to a study, you can influence and distort someone's memory simply by changing the way you ask them a question.

When you want someone to agree with you, be specific and careful with your words. Let's say you're trying to cast suspicion on Blue. Instead of asking if others have seen him (they likely have), ask if others have seen him doing a specific task. Because you're being specific to one task, other crewmates may answer no and forget that Blue may have done other tasks.

It's not a cut-and-dried method. Some may have stronger belief in their memory but identifying who you can easily manipulate can help a lot. It's helpful to plan your questions early on too. Determine how you can be specific without being suspicious.

7. Information manipulation theory: Be economical with the truth

Lies are a lot harder to catch when they're packaged with the truth as indicated by the information manipulation theory. Instead of outright lying, you can opt for incomplete truths by omitting certain facts.

For instance, instead of saying you were in a particular room to distance yourself from a murder, mention how you were nearby without giving any details. So, even if another player is inside that room, you can adapt and claim that you were in the hallway near the room and they may have not seen you. It's also a lot easier to keep your lies intact if you don't provide too much detail.

Be careful not to be too obvious. Interrupting the conversation with meaningless chatter can easily turn the situation against you. Know when to flout and when to obey as others may be adept at recognising lies and untruths.

While these techniques aren't foolproof due to in-game circumstances and group dynamics, it might make it easier to identify an easy scapegoat and score some wins. Do be mindful that Among Us can get pretty intense with all the lying and manipulation, so always check with your friends afterhand to avoid any lingering animosity that may have extended beyond the game.

# IMPOSTORS WILL NOT SEE THIS COMING.

Getting right into it, let's assume you are a crewmate in Among Us. So what is it that a crewmate does exactly? Is it just tasks? Not exactly. After playing Among Us for hours and going from one lobby to another you will inevitably reach the point that tasks are there to keep the player or you in this scenario busy in the game. Is it really surprising that most if not all players want to be impostors all the time? Now, there is nothing wrong with wanting to be an impostor all the time but what if there was a way to ruin all the fun these impostors are having in the game. You'd be surprised at how easy it can be to spot the impostors in the first five minutes of the game.

# The Psychological Mind Games of Among Us

The thing is that any game no matter how good has to have a power balance. In games like COD or PUBG, that balance is achieved by weapons and items having different power scaling. But since Among Us isn't a battle royal game or an FPS shooter it can't create a power balance normally. Instead, what Among Us tries to do is skip power scaling or balancing and instead go for human psychology. Let me explain. If you are a crewmate in Among Us then naturally you will be vary of every other player in the game as they can be the impostor and potentially will kill you. This is critical to understand since impostors behave completely differently.

Impostors in Among Us already know from the moment the game starts who are the other impostors and who are the crewmates. This leads to them responding to the game completely differently. Think of it this way. A crewmate is afraid of the impostor while the impostor is afraid of getting caught. Play it out in your head and you reach the correct conclusion. An impostor is not afraid of crewmates so their responses to emergency meetings or voting or tasks are completely different from a crewmate. Think back to every time you were a ghost in the emergency meetings and how the impostor used to respond every time a dead body was reported.

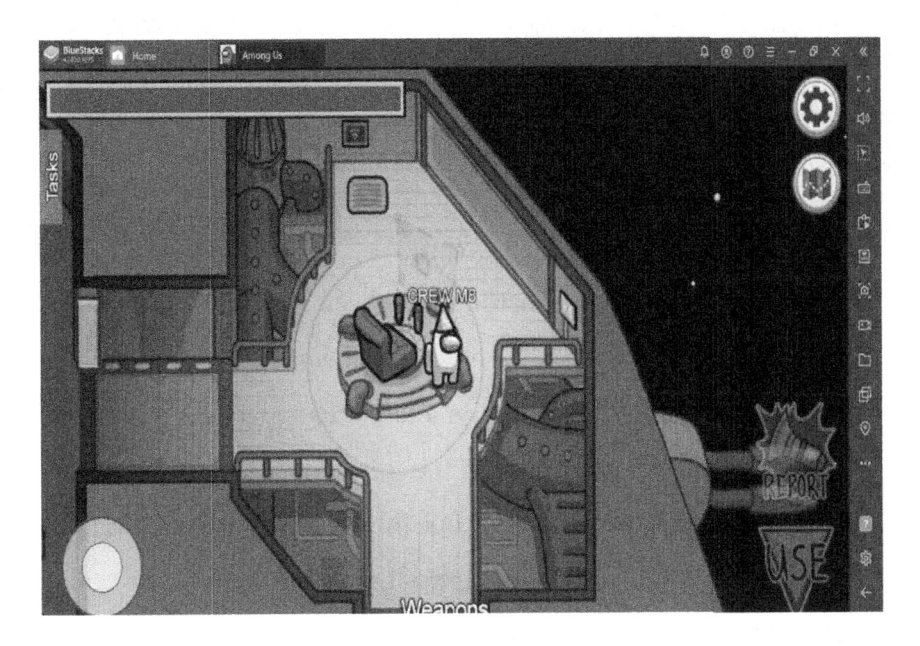

# How to Bamboozle Impostors in Among Us

1. Everyone knows that Impostors fake tasks so that is one way of knowing who the impostor is but knowing is one thing and surprising is another. Every time an emergency meeting is called just write that you know who is the impostor. It is not important that you do know the impostor but the idea itself is scary for the player who is the impostor. It trips them up in most rooms and they will always be on their best behavior since your death will make them the prime suspect.

2. Another thing you can do is write in emergency meetings things like "How did you become the impostor?" without specifying who exactly is the impostor. It has little to no effect on crewmates but what you will get is answers like "You know who is the impostor"

or "tell them who is the killer?" and they will be most of the time from suspected impostors.

3. One thing that many players get frustrated by as Crewmates is the lack of trust among other crewmates. No matter how hard you try you can't make that go away. Try forcing the argument in the emergency meeting and you will be one who gets voted out. So even if you do know the impostor it always helps in making tangible arguments. So avoid using Fake tasks as a valid argument since anyone can say that they were just failing at it. Go for lines like " Major SuS on Green but I'm not sure" even if you are. This makes the argument sound more valid in players' heads which is the real game you need to win.

4. Among us is about mind games but the one who plays them and the one who gets played will always decide the fate of the game. So the next time you want to establish trust among fellow crewmates use lines like "I'm going to security, everyone watch who comes with me". These type of messages in the emergency meetings help players gain trust points which get cashed as soon as you become the impostor. Not only you make yourself but the other player as well be suspect and safe at the same time. So if you die then it was the other player and if the other player dies then it was you who was the impostor.

# Want Voice Chat in Among Us? Play with BlueStacks Then

Everyone knows that games like Among Us are best played with voice chat on but since the game has no voice chat support you have to depend on third-party solutions that are sub-par at best. Even with the best of internet connections, you will experience drops and even random disconnections depending on the ping you get on certain programs. Luckily, BlueStacks Android Emulator devs have done a great job with the new Voice Chat feature that has made playing Among Us amazing for us.

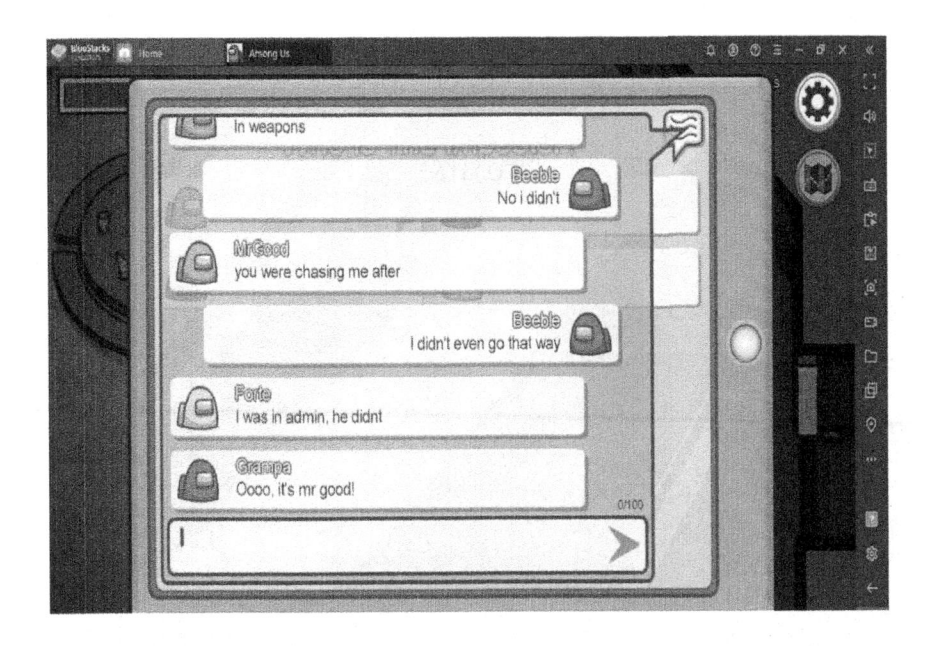

You don't need to download anything for the voice chat feature to work except play Among Us on BlueStacks for free. Among Us is free on Android and with BlueStacks you get the best experience of the game with Keyboard, Mouse, and even gamepad controller support along with voice chat. Just download and install BlueStacks and then install Among Us. That's all you need to do to have everything you need to play the game like your favorite game streamer.

# Among Us: More Important Tips and Tricks for Crewmates and Imposters.

1. Part of the crew

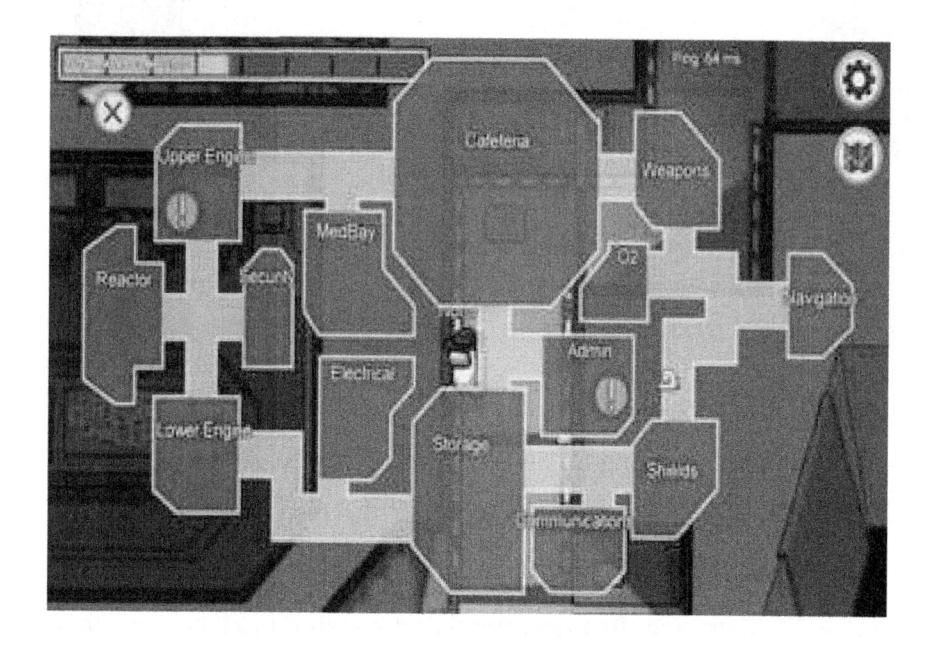

Your priorities as a crewmate are simple: Complete your tasks, fix deadly sabotages, and sniff out imposters without being killed yourself. Or, if you are killed, complete your tasks and trust in your teammates to solve your murder. However, there are particular things you should do to win the game, spot imposters, and avoid falling under suspicion yourself.

I. Remember the tasks you've done

Once a body is discovered, everyone is going to look for the barest hint that someone is lying. So when people ask you where you were and who you were with, be ready to answer quickly, especially if no one was around to corroborate when the discussion begins.

In our Among Us games, when someone is suspicious, saying which room you were in isn't enough. People will ask which tasks you did specifically. So rather than say, "I was in Electrical," it's better to be able to say "I was in Electrical doing wires" or "I was in Storage doing trash." That'll help keep false suspicion off your shoulders.

II. Keep an eye on visual tasks

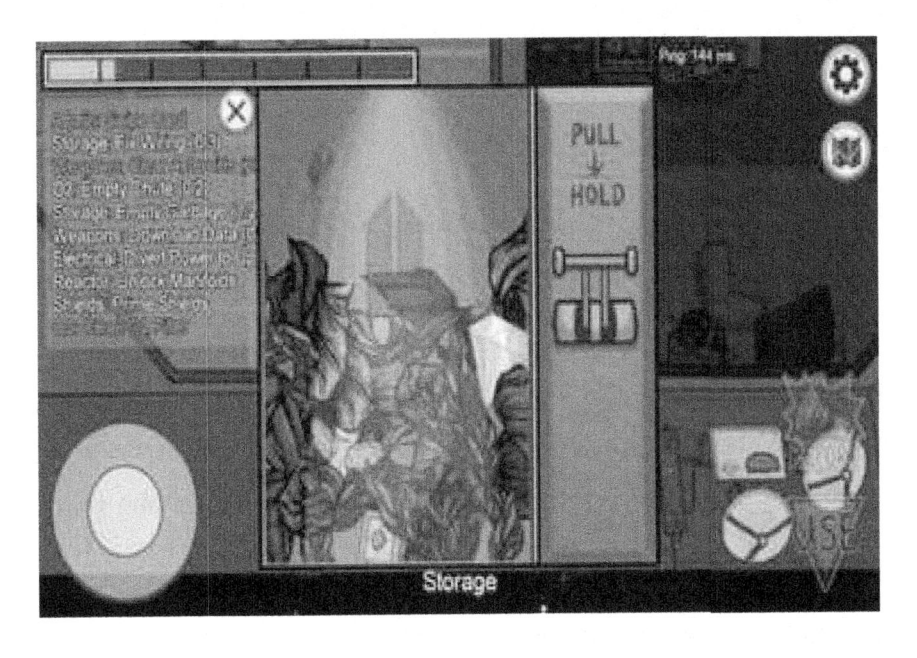

In all three maps, if you perform a Medbay or Laboratory scan, other crewmates can see it, thus proving that you aren't an imposter. That's fairly well known, but you may not know that other tasks can prove innocence or guilt, assuming visual tasks are turned on in the game settings.

In fan-favorite map The Skeld, the empty garbage or empty chute task in Storage visibly causes trash to be vented out into space. In both The Skeld and Polus, the clear asteroids task causes a perceptible laser to appear every time you shoot. Finally, the prime shield task in The Skeld causes lights to turn on outside the ship, or to flicker after a second player completes the task.

If a player stands next to one of these tasks but nothing happens, it's very likely that they are trying to trick you! Or, if you see a visual sign of their innocence, stick to the one person you know you can trust like glue.

III.  Look out for "sus" behavior

When watching your friends in Among Us, it can be difficult to determine if their behavior is innocuous or evil: Is your friend following you because they're doing the buddy system, or because they suspect you, or because they want to kill you? Did they run away from the group to perform a sabotage in private, or because they have one last task to complete? Being creepy in Among Us is kind of unavoidable.

Some behavior is difficult to explain away, however. If a player is standing still, away from any task, right before a sabotage event, that's pretty suspicious. If a crewmate runs into a wall for a few seconds, they may be trying to sabotage while on the move to avoid suspicion. If someone runs behind you only to break off when a third player appears, they clearly were hoping to kill you before realizing there was a witness.

See anything like this, and it may be time to call an emergency meeting.

IV. Don't ghost-watch until you finish tasks

Once you die, it'll be tempting to follow your murderer around and enjoy the show. But do your living teammates a favor and finish off your tasks first. Among Us games are ruined when the living players fix everything against all odds, only to not win and get killed off because their ghost partners didn't bother to finish their tasks out of spite or boredom.

2. You Are An Imposter!

# After a Kill, Find an Alibi

Once a body is reported, crewmates will start by asking "Where?" — meaning where was the body and where was everyone else. If you say you were in the reactor room, only for your friends to say they were there and you weren't, you're basically into the lava already. Wait to hear everyone else's alibis and pick an unoccupied room, and they'll probably find it "sus" that no one else saw you.

That's why, if you have time, you should rush to another room, preferably by vent, and then find a crewmate to hang out with. Once the body is found, you can honestly say, "I was with Red in Electrical." We've found that most people tend to assume a body was found right after the murder, so even if you were with someone for only a short time, people will usually look elsewhere for the imposter.

Or, if you can, lead a crewmate back to your kill. Possibly the most devious trick you can pull off is to kill someone, vent away, pick up a companion, and then lead them back into the room you just left. You'll have an eyewitness who will vouch for you and will have no idea that you would dare return to the scene of the crime.

## TRY BUDDYING UP WITH YOUR FELLOW IMPOSTER

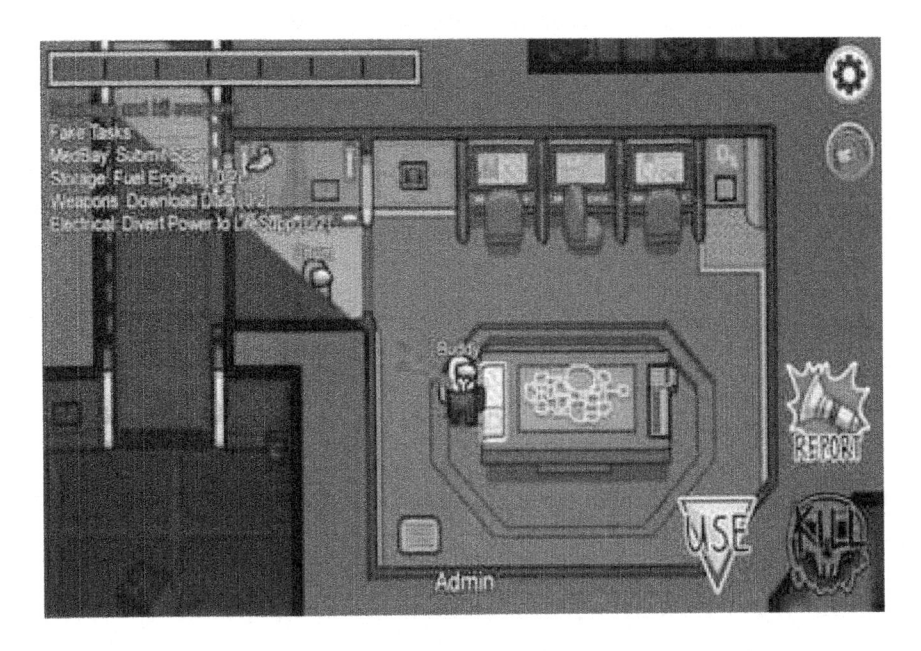

Usually, the smartest play is to split up and pick off crewmates two at a time: Bodies are usually discovered pretty quickly, and each discussion increases the chance that your identity is exposed, so you want to finish them off in batches. On the other hand, hanging out with your fellow imposter can have its perks.

As a crewmate, it's scary when anyone approaches or follows you alone. But if two players approach you, you'll assume that one of them won't kill you with another witness present, and hope that both of them are trustworthy. So, you'll be more likely to accompany them to the more deserted parts of the map.

That's exactly the psychology that you can exploit as an imposter. Join up with your fellow baddie and then run around looking for lone prey. Follow them to a secluded area and kill them, and then you can vouch for each other once the body is discovered. If you're really ambitious, you and your partner can isolate two players at once, wait for them to be occupied with tasks, and then kill them both simultaneously before either knows what's happening.

## Keep Track of the Number of Survivors

The game ends when the crewmates complete the taskbar, or when there are an equal number of crewmates and imposters, since the baddies can no longer be forced out of the airlock. So if you're playing with two imposters, your goal is just to whittle the total number of players down to four. Avoid suspicion for long enough, and if there are just five players left, you can kill someone in full view of the other crewmates — the game will end before they can report.

## Keep Sabotaging as a Ghost

Even after you're caught and killed, an imposter is free to sabotage without worrying about blending in. With your help, the surviving imposter can still pull off a win.

In Among Us late game, the remaining imposter's job becomes much harder: Surviving crewmates who trust one another start to stay in packs, so if someone is killed, the players off on their own get rightfully blamed. And if an imposter kills someone, they're stuck waiting for the kill counter to go down while the good guys get closer to completing tasks. So, your job is to slow down and separate the crewmates, and give your partner time to complete their work.

Most saboteurs go for the flashy attacks like reactor overloads, but don't underestimate locking doors; players will have to wait for at least 10 seconds or flip the door breakers to escape, stalling while your partner's kill cooldown decreases and while crewmates can't move on to the next task. Or, try turning off the lights, which makes it harder to keep track of which players were sticking together when one of them goes missing. Finally, if your partner is down to just a couple of survivors, an emergency meeting could easily expose their lies, so save a sabotage in case you see a player heading toward the big red button.

# KILL IN A CROWD, OR WHEN CREWMATES ARE COMPLETING TASKS

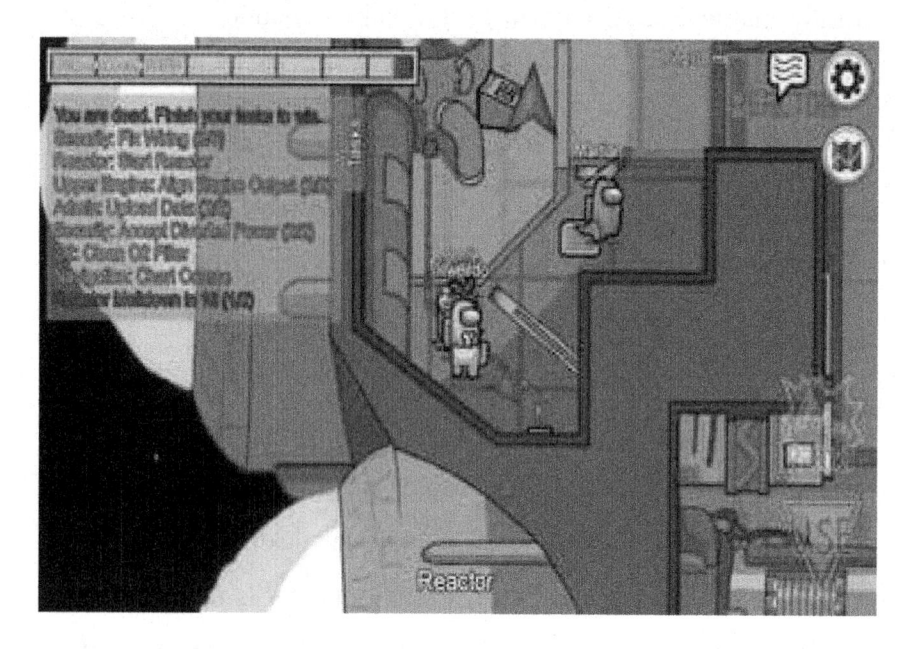

Sometimes, it pays to gamble on a risky kill. Task mini-games take up about 80% of the screen and occupy players' full attention, so even if there are multiple crewmates in a room, you may be able to kill someone and vent away with no one spotting you. Once the surviving crewmate reports the body, they'll end up with no alibi, and crewmates who saw them with the dead teammate will hopefully vote them out too.

In late game, when crewmates are sticking together, a sabotage kill may be your last chance. When everyone heads to Fix Lights or Communications, all the crewmates will be standing on top of one another, desperately flipping switches or turning knobs; stand in the middle of the group, kill a teammate, and stand your ground, and you may find that no one saw who did it, to the exasperation of all the ghosts watching. Even if one person did see you do the deed, you may be able to convince the survivors that "she's the liar, not me!"

## Memorize the Maps' Tasks

As we mentioned above, asking people what tasks they just finished is tricky for imposters, because they haven't been doing tasks! They can say they were in Navigation, but once asked what they've been doing, they'll have to try and remember which tasks are available in that room, and any delay will be pretty suspect.

So as soon as you've killed someone, we recommend putting a mental list together of tasks nearby that you can run off to the crewmates, so they don't suspect you.

3. Who Is The Impostor?

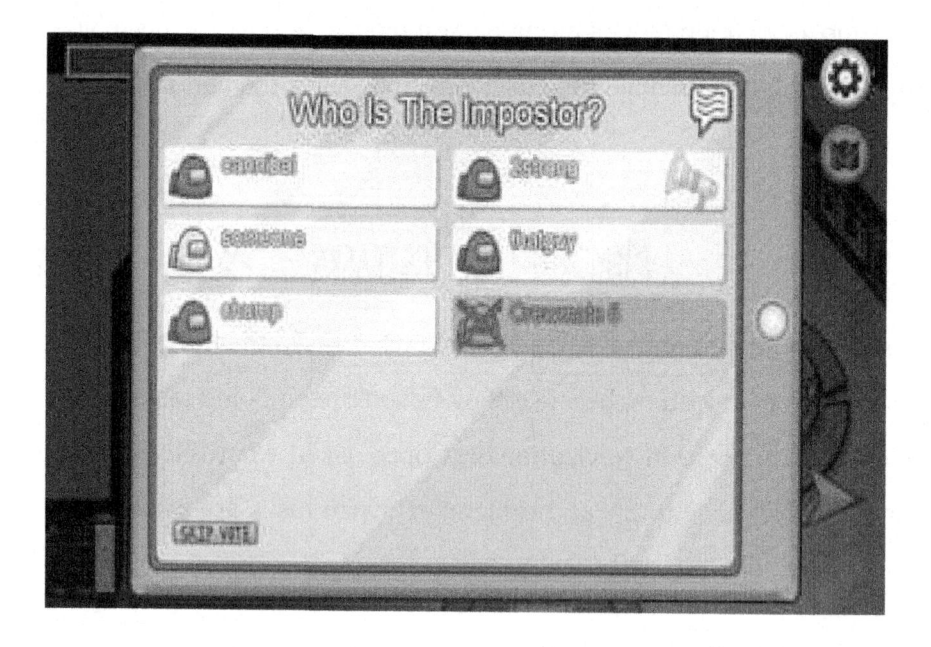

The heart of Among Us, the post-murder discussion is where all of the psychological warfare, interrogations, lying, and ominous "You'll regret this!" pronouncements come into play. Here are our recommendations for spotting lies, fooling your friends, and most important, making Among Us games more fun.

## Play with friends and use Discord

Sometimes, playing with "randos" in Among Us can be fun, but the text discussion menu is slow and unreliable. Everyone spams "where?" after a body is found, then throws out their alibis and accusations. If you're a slow typer, an imposter can announce "Yellow sus" and have people voting for you before you can convince them otherwise. And strangers will often troll by saying they're the imposter to get voted out, simply because they're upset that they weren't picked for imposter.

The optimal way to play Among Us is to jump on a chat with your friends in Discord. Mute when the "Shhhhh" screen appears, then unmute during discussions and listen to your friends' stories. Everyone will have a chance to explain or out themselves, and it's always hilarious when an imposter's alibi is incredibly unconvincing, or when you can get crewmates to question one another instead of you.

# Kick out false accusers

If Cyan swears that she saw Purple jump into a vent, and Purple shoots back that he saw Cyan kill White, you can usually assume that at least one of them is guilty. But if the imposter is trying to trick you into voting an innocent out, your choice is simple – assuming you have Confirm Ejects set to On. Trust the first person to speak up and vote out who they accuse. But if that person turns out to be a crewmate, just wait around the Emergency button until you can call a meeting, and then kick out the false accuser before their kill counter resets.

## BE READY TO BETRAY YOUR FELLOW IMPOSTER

If a crewmate says that they saw Orange kill Blue, and Orange is unconvincing in his defense, the crewmates will unanimously vote him out. You'll be tempted to skip voting or pick someone else in the hopes of saving him, but in doing so you immediately mark yourself as suspicious once they're identified as an imposter.

So, if they're caught, vote them out with no regrets. Better to have one ghost imposter than two. On the other hand, if the debate is less clear-cut and you think the vote could be tight, you can play the "Gosh, I don't know who to vote for!" card and see if the crewmates will give away their opinions before you decide.

# CONCLUSION: WHY AMONG US IS SO SUCCESSFUL.

More than 100 million downloads in September alone with 1.5 million concurrent players, Among us has quickly become a gaming phenomenon. Although the game was released in 2018, it has only attracted rapid popularity recently with unpredictable organic growth.

Among Us has seen a quick rise in popularity due to a combination of multiple factors. It's a unique game with an interesting asymmetrical multiplayer, it's easy to learn thanks to a simple premise, and it's available for (almost) free on a variety of popular platforms, including PC and mobile. But most of all, it's a game that explores new territory: communication and cooperation versus sabotage and deception.

## Mind Games

Here's where the really compelling part comes in. Naturally, the imposter player wants to stick around, murdering the crew until there's only one left and they win. But the rest of the crew doesn't know which of them is the imposter.

So, some creative lying and misdirection are essential for an imposter player to succeed. Imposters often claim to have seen the "real" imposter or suspicious behavior like players crawling through the ventilation (which only the imposter can do). If the imposter can successfully shift the blame to someone else, getting them ejected or sowing enough confusion that no one gets enough votes to be ejected, the game continues.

This is what's so appealing about Among Us: its unique hook pitting a group's teamwork against the deception and manipulation of a human (monster) antagonist. It's a dynamic that really hasn't been explored in a popular video game before ... and which you can expect to see imitated a lot over the next few years.

# A Simple Premise

Among Us is incredibly simple compared to other super-popular games like Fortnite. The graphics are entirely hand-drawn 2D cartoons, you can control your crewmate or imposter character with only a few taps (or the mouse on PC), and even the "repair" mini-games are easy to learn in a few seconds. Players that get "murdered" by the imposter can still help their team, sticking around as ghosts that can complete tasks, but unable to speak during meetings and identify their murderers.

Even so, there are a few ways to improve your play. Remembering the relatively simple map loadouts is important, so you're able to cultivate a sense of situational awareness as a crewmember ... or memorize the best places to hide and ambush people as an imposter.

But the most crucial skill to develop is recognizing patterns of behavior. You'll need to understand the most efficient ways to move around and protect yourself as a crewmember, and the best ways to isolate and strike as an imposter, to be effective on either side.

The game is played with a few variables. Though most people play on the default spaceship level, the Skeld, there are two other maps, a headquarters facility and a polar base inspired by The Thing. You can also set up the game with more than one imposter player. Online multiplayer is the most popular option, with semi-random players, but you can also set up a private game either online or via a local network.

## Explosive Popularity

Among Us was first released in June of 2018, a Unity engine game made by a tiny team of just three developers. It's available as a free mobile game on iOS and Android, and a $5 game on the PC. It had a bit of notoriety and got popular enough for the developers to start working on a sequel.

But it wasn't until a couple of years later that the game started to take off. The key factor: Twitch streamers. The popular live streaming platform saw a boom in players of Among Us, who were fascinated by the social dynamics of the accusation and ejection phase. More streamers hopped on, driving up more and more views.

It helps that the game is free on your phone, so players can hop on and try it out without any commitment. (You can remove the advertising for $2, and buy cute cosmetic "pets" for a few dollars more.) It's also extremely fast: A complete game rarely takes more than 10 minutes, and if you die you can hop into another one almost instantly.

The quick appeal and fascination of Among Us (perhaps spurred on by bored housebound players during the COVID-19 pandemic) has made it a smash hit. It's been downloaded more than 100 million times across its various platforms, with peak player counts claimed at over 1.5 million players. It's developed its own subculture rapidly: If you've heard someone describe shady behavior as "sus," well, now you know where it comes from.

Among Us has grown beyond its initial Twitch audience, appealing especially to younger players. Its simple doodle characters and brutal killing animations have become memes in and of themselves, and it's now spreading into general popular culture. A true cultural cornerstone happened earlier this month, when a U.S. congresswoman played Among Us on Twitch to encourage voter registration for the 2020 election.

While the small developer team InnerSloth had intended to create a more complex sequel to Among Us, the exploding popularity of the game has taxed its resources. It will be working on improving the current game for the time being, adding more robust account and friend support, new stages, and better accessibility for colorblind players. Perhaps most crucially, more servers will be added to keep up with demand.

Like Fortnite and Fall Guys, you can expect to see a lot of imitators for Among Us on PCs, consoles, and especially mobile phones in the near future. Be wary of these: the game has an extremely reasonable monetization setup with no pay-to-win features, which is rare for a mobile game. Others may not be so reserved.

Among Us 2 is cancelled for the time being, but it seems unlikely that it's been completely scrapped. Expect work on a sequel or follow-up of some kind to resume once the team can stabilize and streamline the current game ... and perhaps when they stop seeing millions of concurrent players.

Made in the USA
Monee, IL
26 March 2021